How to Draw the Life and Times of
Franklin Delano Roosevelt

Melody S. Mis

The Rosen Publishing Group's
PowerKids Press™
New York

To my cousin, Bill Heavener, for his wisdom and his tender heart

Published in 2006 by The Rosen Publishing Group, Inc.
29 East 21st Street, New York, NY 10010

First Edition

Editor: Jennifer Way
Layout Design: Ginny Chu
Photo Researcher: Amy Feinberg

Illustration Credits: All illustrations by Michelle Innes.
Photo Credits: pp. 4, 12 © Corbis; pp. 7, 22 (left) © Bettmann/Corbis; p. 8 Cindy Reiman; p. 9 Michael Reed/www.thecemeteryproject.com; p. 10 © Walter Sanders/Time Life Pictures/Getty Images; p. 14 © Alan Schein Photography/Corbis; pp. 16, 20 Franklin D. Roosevelt Library Digital Archives; p. 18 Library of Congress Prints and Photographs Division; p. 22 (right) National Museum of American History, Smithsonian Institution; p. 24 NPS/USS Arizona Memorial Photo Collection; p. 26 © Clive Newton/The Military Picture Library/Corbis; p. 28 White House Historical Association (White House Collection).

Library of Congress Cataloging-in-Publication Data

Mis, Melody S.
How to draw the life and times of Franklin Delano Roosevelt / Melody S. Mis.— 1st ed.
p. cm. — (A kid's guide to drawing the presidents of the United States of America) Includes index.
ISBN 1-4042-3008-4 (library binding)
1. Roosevelt, Franklin D. (Franklin Delano), 1882–1945—Juvenile literature. 2. Presidents—United States—Biography—Juvenile literature. 3. Drawing—Technique—Juvenile literature. I. Title. II. Series.
E807.M57 2006
973.917'092—dc22

2005007737

Printed in China

Contents

Franklin Delano Roosevelt

Franklin Delano Roosevelt was one of America's greatest presidents. He helped the nation through the Great Depression and guided the country during World War II. He was the only president to have been elected to four terms in office.

Franklin D. Roosevelt was born on January 30, 1882, in Hyde Park, New York. His parents, James and Sara Delano Roosevelt, were well known in New York. James was vice president of the Delaware & Hudson Railway.

In 1900, Roosevelt entered Harvard University in Cambridge, Massachusetts. From 1904 to 1907, he studied law at Columbia University in New York City. Around this time he met Eleanor Roosevelt, a distant cousin, whom he married. They had six children.

In 1910, Roosevelt was nominated by the Democratic Party to run for the New York senate. He won the election and was reelected in 1912. In 1913, he was appointed the assistant secretary of the

U.S. Navy, a post he held until 1920. In 1921, he became sick with polio, which paralyzed him from the waist down. Eleanor encouraged him to continue his work in politics.

In 1928, Roosevelt was elected governor of New York. During both of his two-year terms as governor, Roosevelt created programs that gave jobs to many people who had lost their jobs during the Great Depression. The Democratic Party noticed Roosevelt's success as governor and nominated him for president in the 1932 election. He won the election and became the thirty-second president.

You will need the following supplies to draw the life and times of Franklin D. Roosevelt:

✓ A sketch pad   ✓ An eraser   ✓ A pencil   ✓ A ruler

These are some of the shapes and drawing terms you need to know:

Horizontal Line	——	Squiggly Line	∿
Oval	⬭	Trapezoid	⏢
Rectangle	▭	Triangle	△
Shading	▰	Vertical Line	|
Slanted Line	/	Wavy Line	∿

The Thirty-second President

Franklin Roosevelt was sworn into office on March 4, 1933, during the Great Depression. Roosevelt tried to comfort Americans by telling them that "the only thing we have to fear is fear itself." He spent the first 100 days in office trying to help people affected by the Great Depression. He established programs that helped create jobs. These programs were part of his plan called the New Deal.

Americans felt that Roosevelt's New Deal was helping them, and they elected him to three more four-year terms. It was the only time in American history that a president was elected to four terms. In 1939, during Roosevelt's second term, World War II began in Europe. America entered the war in 1941, after Japan attacked U.S. ships stationed at Pearl Harbor in Hawaii.

During the next three years, Roosevelt led the nation through the war. Near the end of the war, Roosevelt became sick. He died on April 12, 1945, just four months before the war ended on August 14, 1945.

In this picture Roosevelt is shown at the Yalta Conference. The conference was a 1945 meeting of the Allied leaders at which they planned to end World War II. Seated left to right are British prime minister Winston Churchill, U.S. president Roosevelt, and Soviet premier Joseph Stalin.

Roosevelt's New York

The Franklin D. Roosevelt Presidential Library opened in 1941.

New York

Map of the United States of America

Franklin Roosevelt spent most of his life in New York. He was born in Hyde Park, had a law office in New York City, and served in Albany as a state senator and as governor. Today New York honors Roosevelt by maintaining his presidential library, located on the grounds of Springwood, his home at Hyde Park.

The Franklin D. Roosevelt Presidential Library was the nation's first presidential library and the only one to be used by a president while he was in office. Roosevelt designed the library in 1939. The library was built to store his papers, presidential gifts, and other articles of historical importance. It was from the library's study that Roosevelt sometimes gave the radio talks known as Fireside Chats.

Today the library is a museum that includes such exhibits as the toy ships he built, the desk he used when he was president, and a wheelchair that he designed. Also on display is the Ford automobile that was made especially for Roosevelt. It was operated by hand levers, which made it easy for him to drive after he had lost the use of his legs.

Franklin Roosevelt is buried at Springwood in Hyde Park, New York. This is on the same grounds as his former home and the presidential museum.

When Roosevelt died on April 12, 1945, he was buried in the rose garden near his presidential library. A white marble monument and the American flag mark his grave.

Springwood

Franklin Roosevelt was born at Springwood, the family home in Hyde Park, New York, on January 30, 1882. Roosevelt was happy at Springwood. As a

child he was interested in trees and planted many of those that still stand on the grounds today.

After Roosevelt and Eleanor married in 1905, they moved in with his widowed mother at Springwood. In 1915, Roosevelt added onto the house, turning it into a 35-room mansion. He loved Springwood and entertained many important people there. The most famous people to visit Springwood were King George VI and Queen Elizabeth of Great Britain in 1939.

After Roosevelt died in 1945, Springwood was opened to the public as a museum, as he had requested. The home includes things such as Roosevelt's stamp and bird collections and the chair in which his Scottish terrier dog, Fala, slept.

1

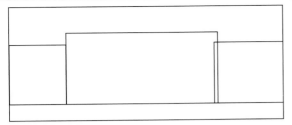

Begin drawing Springwood with a rectangular guide. Inside this guide draw three rectangles. Notice that the rectangle on the right overlaps the middle one.

2

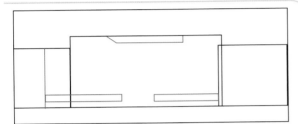

Add more guides by making two rectangles and several slanted lines as shown. These guides will help you draw the many levels of the front of Springwood.

3

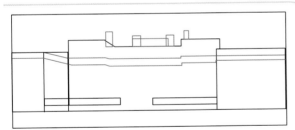

Erase extra lines. Add more rectangles to the roof. These will be the chimneys. Draw a line across the front of the building exactly like the one above it and a vertical line on the left.

4

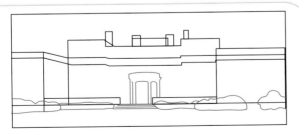

Draw an entryway with columns. Connect them with a curved top. Add steps below this shape. Add bushes with wavy lines.

5

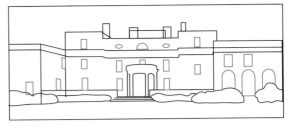

Erase extra line. Add windows all over the building. Notice some windows are rectangles and some have curved tops. There are also two small oval windows above the entrance.

6

Erase extra lines. Add lines to the windows. Next add many small vertical lines to the rail in front of and on top of the house.

7

Draw the front door. Notice that it is slightly hidden behind the entrance. Finish drawing the house by adding trees, plants, and some details to the house.

8

Shade the drawing. You can add the ivy and bricks with shading. You can add the leaves to the front trees as well. Well done!

Meet Eleanor Roosevelt

Anna Eleanor Roosevelt was born on October 11, 1884, in New York City to Elliot and Anna Hall Roosevelt. By the time Eleanor was 10 years old, both of her parents had died, and she went to live in New York City with her grandmother.

In 1903, she began working with poor young people in New York City. It was during this time that she met Franklin Roosevelt, whom she married in 1905. Eleanor helped Roosevelt campaign for the many offices he held during his lifetime. When he became ill with polio in 1921, Eleanor helped him get back to working in politics.

After Roosevelt was elected president in 1933, Eleanor took an active part as First Lady. For example, she occasionally held women-only press conferences, which she hoped would encourage newspapers to hire women reporters. When Eleanor died of a lung illness on November 7, 1962, she was buried beside Roosevelt at Springwood.

1

Begin your picture of Eleanor Roosevelt by drawing two ovals inside a rectangle. The ovals will be guides for drawing her head and her shoulders.

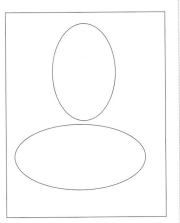

2

Using wavy lines draw the hair around the outside of the head guide. Next draw the outline of the shoulders and neck around the oval guide below.

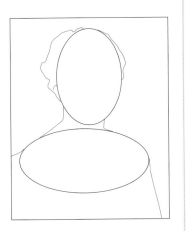

3

Draw the front of the hair by drawing wavy lines. Add the shape of the dress, her right arm, and her clothes using slanted and curved lines.

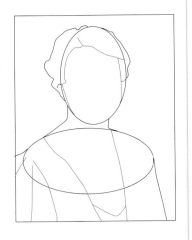

4

Erase the oval guides. Add two crossing straight lines on the face oval. These will be guides for drawing her face. Add her pearl necklace by drawing many small circles.

5

Using the guides you drew in step 4, draw the face as shown. Use the horizontal guide for the placement of the eyes. Try not to outline the features completely.

6

Erase the face guides and finish the portrait with shading. You can add the rest of the detail in the face and in the pattern of her dress using shading. Add as much as you can. Great job!

The New York Senate

In 1910, Franklin Roosevelt campaigned for the New York senate. The Democratic Party believed Roosevelt could win the election, because his family was  well known. His distant cousin Theodore Roosevelt had been president of the United States.

After Franklin Roosevelt won the election, he worked in Albany's capitol building, shown here. While he was in office, Roosevelt worked hard to rid the state government of politicians who had taken money in exchange for political favors.

During his senate career, Roosevelt supported women's right to vote and a six-day workweek. At that time many companies required their workers to work seven days a week. Roosevelt was so popular with New Yorkers that he was elected for a second term. He served in the senate until 1913, when President Woodrow Wilson appointed him assistant secretary of the navy.

1

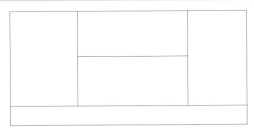

Begin drawing the New York capitol by creating guides. Draw a large rectangle with two horizontal lines and two vertical lines as shown.

2

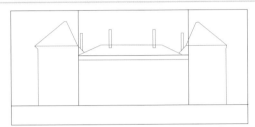

Draw the roof by making two triangular shapes and three lines. Draw four chimneys and connect them to the roof lines. Add two lines on either side of the building.

3

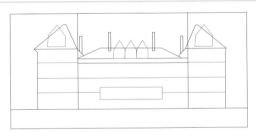

Add horizontal lines to the building. Add a rectangle in the middle of the building. Draw the shapes on the roof as shown.

4

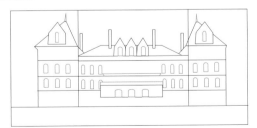

Erase extra lines. Add windows by drawing many arches. Add a small, thin shape on either side of the roof. Draw the lines in the center of the building as shown.

5

Draw more lines in the center of the building as shown. Add more windows using rectangles and arches. Next draw the slanted lines at the bottom of the building.

6

Erase extra guidelines. Draw horizontal lines for the stairs. Add railings on either side of the stairs. Next add details to the roof using small vertical lines and two slanted lines to the towers.

7

Erase extra lines. Using vertical and slanted lines, add detail to the railing and to the roof of the building. Then add two flags to the roof. Finish adding details to the building as shown.

8

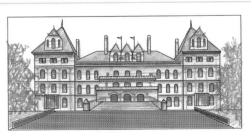

Use shading to add as much detail to the capitol building as you can. Add trees and bushes next to the building. Wonderful job!

Roosevelt and Polio

In 1920, Franklin Roosevelt left his post as assistant secretary of the U.S. Navy and returned to New York City, where he practiced law. During the summer of 1921, the 39-year-old Roosevelt became ill with polio. His legs were paralyzed. He

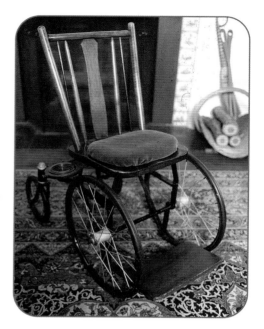

learned how to use a wheelchair and how to walk short distances by wearing heavy leg braces and using crutches. He also built his own wheelchairs, like the one shown here. After a few years, Roosevelt felt healthy enough to return to politics. He ran for governor of New York in 1928 and won the election.

Roosevelt wanted to help other people with polio. In 1927, he bought a health center in Warm Springs, Georgia. In 1938, he founded the March of Dimes, an organization that supported medical studies to find a cure for polio. In 1997, Washington, D.C., honored the former president for his courage in living with a disability by placing a statue of him in his wheelchair at the Franklin D. Roosevelt Memorial.

1 Begin drawing the wheelchair with a rectangular guide. Add three angled lines to the inside of the rectangle.

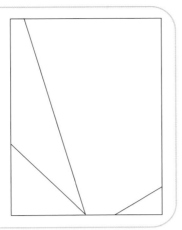

2 Next draw three ovals. The two larger ones are the front wheels and the smaller one is the back wheel. Draw two angled lines at the bottom right for the footrest.

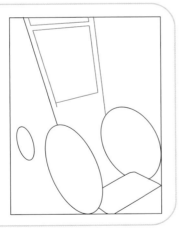

3 Erase the lines that go through the wheels. To draw the back of the wheelchair add slanted lines.

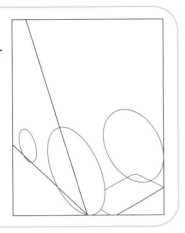

4 Add the slats to the back of the chair with two wavy lines in the center and slanted lines on either side. Draw the seat and the seat cushion by making the shapes shown.

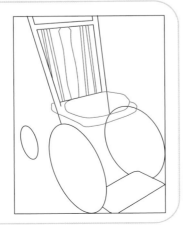

5 Erase extra lines around the seat and cushion. Using ovals and lines, add the axles that connect the wheels to each other and to the chair.

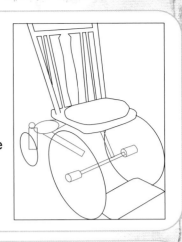

6 Continue by drawing the inside rims of the wheels. Add the spokes of the wheels with many slanted lines.

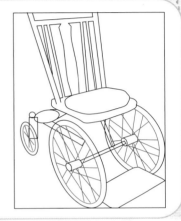

7 Erase the large rectangular guide and other extra lines. Add handles to the back of the wheelchair using curved and squiggly lines. Add a line around the seat of the chair.

8 Add detail and shading to the wheelchair. The wheels and gears can be filled in completely. Great work!

Governor of New York

In 1928, Franklin Roosevelt won the election for governor of New York. During his campaign and for the rest of his public life, Roosevelt asked that he not be

pictured in such a way that it showed his disability. Roosevelt was afraid people would think that he was unable to do the job because he was disabled.

Roosevelt won the election and in 1929 he returned to Albany. While he was governor of New York, he lived in the Executive Mansion, shown here. During Roosevelt's four years as governor, his biggest success was his plan to provide jobs and unemployment insurance for New Yorkers who had lost their jobs during the Great Depression. He was convinced that he could use his ideas to help the whole nation recover from the Depression. When the national Democratic Party asked Roosevelt to run for president in 1932, he accepted.

1

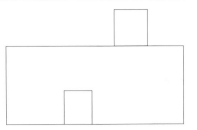

Begin drawing the Executive Mansion by making three rectangles as shown. These will be guides for the building.

2

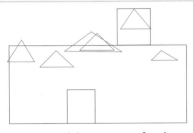

Draw the many gables or roof edges on the house by adding six triangles as shown. Gables are triangular roof edges.

3

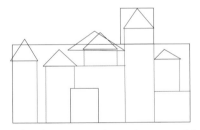

Next draw the horizontal and vertical lines that appear on the face of the building. These will become the many sections of the house.

4

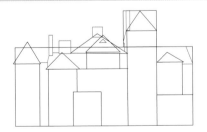

Add four chimneys to the roof using rectangles. Draw a small triangle in the center gable. Add lines to connect the gables and make the main roof of the house as shown.

5

Erase extra lines. Next add the windows on the front of the building by making many small rectangles.

6

Add more detail to the building. Notice that there is an arched doorway and a larger arched window.

7

Erase the extra guidelines. Finish drawing the building by adding the door and the steps. Add trees and bushes in front of the house.

8

Erase extra lines around the trees and bushes. Shade as much detail in the building as you can and you're finished!

The New Deal

Franklin Roosevelt was the Democratic candidate to run against President Herbert Hoover in the 1932 election. Hoover did not believe it was the government's duty to help Americans who were suffering during the Great Depression. Roosevelt, however, believed

A MESSAGE OF HOPE

that the government should help its citizens. During his campaign Roosevelt promised Americans a new deal to help the nation. This New Deal was talked about in newspapers and in political cartoons, such as the one shown here. Roosevelt won the election on the strength of his New Deal plans.

After Roosevelt took office on March 4, 1933, he began to put his New Deal into action. Under the New Deal, people were hired to construct bridges, roads, and public buildings. The New Deal also established a minimum wage for workers. These New Deal projects improved the country while putting people to work, which gave Americans hope.

1

Begin the cartoon by drawing a large rectangle with a smaller one inside it. Draw a horizontal line at the top of the large rectangle. These will be your guides.

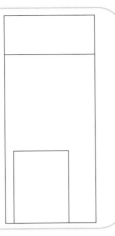

2

Draw the outline of the plane. Use an oval to show the propeller, a rectangular shape for the wings, and a curved shape for the body of the plane.

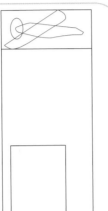

3

Erase extra lines. Add the name "ROOSEVELT" under the wings. Draw the tail of the plane as shown and two circles for the wheels. Add some lines to the propeller to make it look like it is spinning.

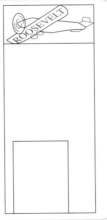

4

Erase the horizontal line. Halfway down add the shape shown for the letter. Write the words "I PLEDGE YOU – I PLEDGE MYSELF – TO A NEW DEAL FOR THE AMERICAN PEOPLE."

5

Erase the large rectangle. Begin drawing the man and woman by adding guides. Use circles for their heads and slanted lines for their bodies.

6

Draw the woman first. Use the guides to outline her dress, apron, arms, and hands.

7

Erase extra lines. Draw the man, including his clothing. Draw the label attached to the man and write the words "THE FORGOTTEN MAN" in it. Add the outline of hair to the man and woman.

8

Erase the extra guides and begin shading. Great job!

Roosevelt's Fireside Chats

Franklin Roosevelt understood that the nation's problems during the Great Depression had made Americans  fearful. He hoped that he could ease their fears by telling them what he and the government were doing to help them.

In the 1930s, nearly every home in America had a radio. Throughout his presidency Roosevelt broadcast speeches that he called Fireside Chats. He made these speeches from either the White House or his home in Hyde Park. Roosevelt used a microphone, like the one shown here, to record and broadcast his chats. It was the first time that a president regularly used the radio as a way to talk to the country.

Roosevelt's success in using the radio to talk to Americans encouraged other politicians to use it to campaign for government offices. His Fireside Chats also became a model for the way presidents today use radio and television to talk about their programs.

1

To begin drawing the microphone, make a rectangular guide. Draw an oval at the bottom of the rectangular guide. This will become the base of the microphone.

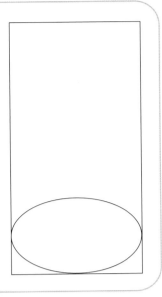

2

Add another rectangle inside the rectangle you drew in step 1. Outline the bottom of the base of the microphone with a wavy line. Add a semicircle and two curved lines to the inside of the base. On top of the curved lines, draw a small oval that overlaps the rectangle.

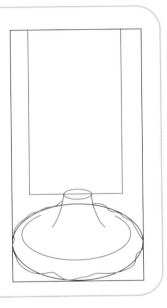

3

Continue by drawing another two shapes connected to it. This will be the main part of the microphone.

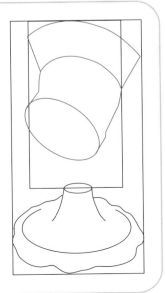

4

Erase extra lines. Add the details to the microphone by drawing an oval inside the oval you drew in step 3. Draw the lines above the oval. Add a shape to the right of the microphone.

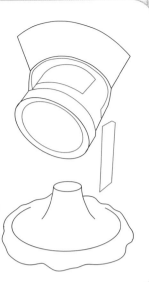

5

Now draw the lines that connect the microphone to its base. Draw the lines on either side of the microphone. Write the letters "NBC" on top of the microphone and on its side.

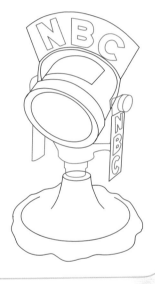

6

Finish your drawing with shading. Shade the microphone very dark and leave the letters "NBC" light. Great job!

World War II

During Franklin Roosevelt's second term as president, World War II began between the Axis powers and  the Allied powers. The Axis powers were Germany, Italy, and Japan. France and Great Britain were the main Allied powers. In 1939, Germany attacked Poland. The United States stayed neutral because Roosevelt had promised not to make Americans fight in a foreign war.

On December 7, 1941, Japan attacked American ships at Pearl Harbor in Hawaii. They sunk 12 ships, including the USS *Arizona*, shown here. Roosevelt said that that terrible day would "live in infamy." The next day the United States joined the Allies and entered the war.

Americans came together in support of the war. The Allies won the war, which ended on August 14, 1945. Roosevelt did not live to enjoy this victory, because he died just four months before the war's end.

1

Begin drawing the USS *Arizona* by making a rectangular guide. Add a horizontal line to the inside of the rectangle, near the bottom.

2

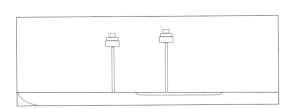

Next draw the two masts in the middle of the ship. Draw three stacked rectangles at the top of each mast. Add the curves to the hull, or body, of the ship as shown.

3

Erase extra lines. Add the shapes of the ship's guns and hold using curved shapes. Add rectangles, too. Now draw the water hitting the front of the ship using a wavy line.

4

Erase extra lines. Now you can add the shape shown using many straight and curved lines.

5

Add shapes to the right side of the ship using straight and slanted lines.

6

Next draw the three planes on the right side of the ship. Add the details to the ship's masts. Notice there are flags at the top of each mast.

7

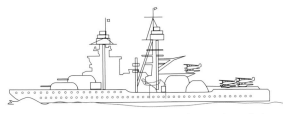

Draw a small rescue boat on the side of the ship. You can add windows to the ship's hull by drawing many small circles. Draw a wavy line for the water's surface.

8

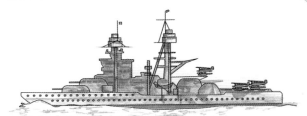

Finish by shading the ship. Add as much detail as you can. Wonderful job!

The United Nations

While World War II was being fought in Europe, Roosevelt created a plan for a peacekeeping organization. His plan had begun in 1941, when he and Britain's prime

minister, Winston Churchill, wrote the Atlantic Charter. The charter stated rules that countries would have to follow to settle arguments peacefully. The 26 Allied countries adopted the charter the following year.

In 1944, the leaders from the United States, Great Britain, the Soviet Union, and China met in Washington, D.C., to create a peacekeeping organization. They called this group the United Nations, a name that Roosevelt had suggested. The United Nations's flag is shown here.

Unfortunately, Roosevelt died in April 1945, six months before the United Nations was officially established. Each October 24, United Nations Day is celebrated to honor the day that the organization was officially founded.

1

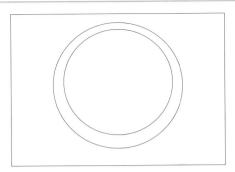

Begin drawing the United Nations flag by making a rectangular guide. Add two circle guides, one inside the other. Notice that the smaller circle is slightly off center.

2

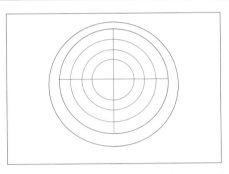

Next draw three circles inside the small circle you drew in step 1. Notice that each circle is smaller than the next. Add two lines, one vertical and one horizontal, that cross in the middle.

3

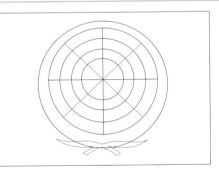

Add two diagonal lines that also cross in the center of the smallest circle. Begin drawing the decorative olive branches by adding the shapes at the bottom of the largest circle. Olive branches represent peace.

4

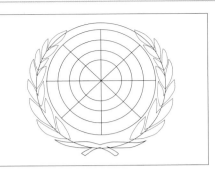

Follow the large circle guide and add more leaves to the olive branches. Each side has the same number of leaves.

5

Erase the outer circle guide. Next draw the shapes of the world's continents. Notice that you are looking at the top of Earth so the continent shapes look different.

6

Erase the lines inside the continents and in the center of the circles. Shade the flag. Good job, you're finished!

Roosevelt's Legacy

Franklin Roosevelt died suddenly from a brain hemorrhage on April 12, 1945, in Warm Springs, Georgia. He was 63 years old. When people heard the news of his death on the radio, they were shocked and saddened.

As Roosevelt's funeral train began its journey north to Washington, D.C., thousands of people lined the railroad tracks at towns along the way. After the president's memorial service at the White House, he was buried at Hyde Park.

Roosevelt is remembered as a great president. He led the nation through the Great Depression and World War II, and he helped create the United Nations. Some of his New Deal programs are still helping people today. Roosevelt's courage in dealing with polio inspired people and made them believe they could overcome their problems. Roosevelt was such an important leader that some historians rank him as the third-greatest American president, behind George Washington and Abraham Lincoln.

1

Begin drawing the portrait of Roosevelt by drawing a rectangle. Add a rectangle inside it as a guide for his body. Add an oval as the guide for his head. Draw a slanted line as a guide for his left arm.

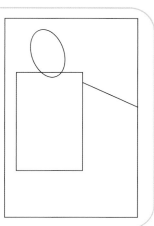

2

Start outlining the shapes of the arms with wavy lines. Remember to follow the guides you drew in step 1.

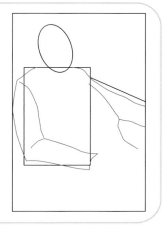

3

Continue outlining the jacket with the shapes of the collar and necktie. Next draw the shape of the head and hair. Use the oval guide to add the shape of the profile.

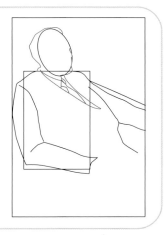

4

Erase extra guidelines. Finish his clothes by adding the rest of the lapels and his shirt cuff. Add a shape for the handkerchief in the jacket pocket. Draw an oval as a guide for the hand.

5

Now draw the hand. Follow the oval guide. Notice that only four fingers are showing. Next draw the shape of the armchair where Roosevelt's arm is resting.

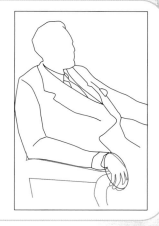

6

Erase the hand oval. Add guides for the face. Draw a curved line for the chin and another curved line for the ear. Use a wavy line to show the hairline. Add folds to the jacket.

7

Look closely at the photo to draw the eyes, nose, and mouth. Draw the lines that outline the shape of the cheek and the shadow under the bottom line.

8

Erase the face guides. Finally shade the drawing to finish. Notice that the suit is very dark. Great job!

Timeline

1882   Franklin Delano Roosevelt is born on January 30.

1900–1904   Roosevelt attends Harvard University.

1904–1907   Roosevelt studies law at Columbia University.

1905   Eleanor Roosevelt and Franklin Roosevelt marry.

1911–1913   Roosevelt is a New York state senator.

1913–1920   Woodrow Wilson appoints Roosevelt as assistant secretary of the U.S. Navy.

1921   While on vacation, Roosevelt becomes ill with polio.

1927   Roosevelt buys a health retreat in Warm Springs, Georgia.

1928   Roosevelt is elected governor of New York.

1932   Roosevelt is elected the thirty-second president of the United States.

1933   Roosevelt passes his New Deal program in the first 100 days. Roosevelt begins his Fireside Chats.

1936   Roosevelt is reelected for his second term.

1939   World War II begins in Europe.

1940   Roosevelt is elected president for his third term.

1941   The Japanese bomb Pearl Harbor. The United States enters World War II.

1944   Roosevelt is reelected for his fourth term.

1945   Franklin Delano Roosevelt dies on April 12. World War II ends on August 14.

Glossary

braces (BRAYS-ez) Something that provides support to a body part.

broadcast (BROD-kast) To put something on television or radio.

designed (dih-ZYND) Drew or planned something.

foreign (FOR-in) Outside one's own country.

Great Depression (GRAYT dih-PREH-shun) A period of American history during the late 1920s and early 1930s. Banks and businesses lost money and there were few jobs.

hemorrhage (HEM-rij) Uncontrollable bleeding from blood vessels.

infamy (IN-fuh-mee) Shame, dishonor.

insurance (in-SHUR-ints) Protection against loss or harm.

legacy (LEH-guh-see) Something left behind by a person's actions.

levers (LEH-vurz) Handles.

mansion (MAN-shun) A very large house, often with a lot of land surrounding it.

memorial (meh-MOR-ee-ul) Something used as a reminder of a person, a place, or an event.

minimum wage (MIH-nih-mum WAYJ) The lowest salary that a worker can legally be paid.

neutral (NOO-trul) On neither side of an argument or war.

nominated (NAH-muh-nayt-ed) Selected to do a certain job.

paralyzed (PER-uh-lyzd) To have lost feeling or movement in the limbs.

pledge (PLEJ) A promise or agreement.

polio (POH-lee-oh) A once-common illness that sometimes caused loss of movement in certain muscles.

prime minister (PRYM MIH-neh-ster) The leader of a government.

unemployment (un-im-PLOY-ment) Having to do with being without a job.

widowed (WIH-dohd) Having to do with a woman whose husband has died.

World War II (WURLD WOR TOO) A war fought by the United States, Great Britain, France, and the Soviet Union against Germany, Japan, and Italy from 1939 to 1945.

Index

Web Sites

Due to the changing nature of Internet links, PowerKids Press has developed an online list of Web sites related to the subject of this book. This site is updated regularly. Please use this link to access the list:
www.powerkidslinks.com/kgdpusa/froosevelt/